DISCIPLES PATH
for students

THE
WAY

DISCOVERING CHRIST'S
PATH OF DISCIPLESHIP

LifeWay Press®
Nashville, Tennessee

LifeWay | Students

DISCIPLES PATH
for students

Disciples Path is a series of resources founded on Jesus' model of discipleship. Created by experienced disciple-makers across the nation, it offers an intentional pathway for transformational discipleship and a way to help followers of Christ move from new disciples to mature disciple-makers. Each resource in the series is built around the principles of modeling, practicing, and multiplying:

- Leaders model the life of a biblical disciple.

- Disciples follow and practice from the leader.

- Disciples become disciple-makers and multiply through the *Disciples Path.*

Each study in the series has been written and approved by disciple-makers for small groups and one-on-one settings.

Contributors:
Eddy Pearson, the Arizona Southern Baptist Convention
Ben Reed, Saddleback Church, Lake Forest, California

Item: 005773607
ISBN: 9781430051671
Dewey decimal classification number: 248.84
Subject heading: DISCIPLESHIP \ JESUS CHRIST \ CHRISTIAN LIFE

Eric Geiger
Vice President, Church Resources

Rick Howerton
Discipleship Specialist

Sam O'Neal, Joel Polk, Karen Daniel
Content Editors

Ben Trueblood
Director, Student Ministry

Chris Swain
Manager, Student Ministry Publishing

We believe that the Bible has God for its author; salvation for its end; and truth, without any mixture of error, for its matter and that all Scripture is totally true and trustworthy. To review LifeWay's doctrinal guideline, please visit *www.lifeway.com/doctrinalguideline.*

Unless otherwise noted, all Scripture quotations are taken from the Holman Christian Standard Bible®, copyright 1999, 2000, 2002, 2003, 2009 by Holman Bible Publishers. Used by permission.

For ordering or inquiries, visit www.lifeway.com; write LifeWay Students; One LifeWay Plaza; Nashville, TN 37234-0144; or call toll free (800) 458-2772.

Printed in the United States of America.

Student Ministry Publishing
LifeWay Resources
One LifeWay Plaza
Nashville, Tennessee 37234-0144

Cover photo and illustrations: Thinkstock

CONTENTS

A NOTE FOR DISCIPLE-MAKERS

Several years ago I was a part of a massive research study that sought to discover how the Lord often brings about transformation in the hearts of His people. The study became a book called *Transformational Discipleship*. Basically, we wanted to learn how disciples are made. Based on study of Scripture and lots of interactions with people, we concluded that transformation is likely to occur when a godly **leader** applies **truth** to the heart of a person while that person is in a teachable **posture**.

- **Leader:** You are the leader. As you invest in the students you're discipling, they will learn much about the Christian faith by watching you, by sensing your heart for the Lord, and by seeing you pursue Him. I encourage you to seek to be the type of leader that can say, "Follow my example as I follow the example of Christ."

- **Truth:** These studies were developed in deep collaboration with ministry leaders who regularly and effectively disciple people. The studies are designed to take the students you disciple into the Word of God—because we're confident that Jesus and His Word sanctify us and transform us. Our community of disciple-makers mapped out a path of the truths we believe are essential for each believer to know and understand.

- **Posture:** Hopefully the students you will be investing in adopt a teachable posture—one that is open and hungry for the Lord. Encourage them to take the study seriously and to view your invitation to study together as a sacred opportunity to experience the grace of God and the truth of God.

We hope and pray the Lord will use this study in your life and the lives of those you disciple. As you apply the truth of God to teachable hearts, transformation will occur. Thank you for being a disciple-maker!

In Christ,

Eric

Eric Geiger
Vice President at LifeWay Christian Resources
Co-author of *Transformational Discipleship*

WHAT IS A DISCIPLE?

Congratulations! If you've chosen to live as a disciple of Jesus, you've made the most important decision imaginable. But you may be wondering, *What does it mean to be a disciple?*

To put it simply, a disciple of Jesus is someone who has chosen to follow Jesus. That's the command Jesus gave to those He recruited as His first disciples: "Follow me." In Jesus' culture, religious leaders called rabbis would gather a group of followers, called disciples, to follow in their footsteps and learn their teachings. In the same way, you will become more and more like Jesus as you purposefully follow Him in the weeks to come. Jesus once said, "Everyone who is fully trained will be like his teacher" (Luke 6:40).

On a deeper level, disciples of Jesus are those learning to base their identities on Jesus Himself. All of us use different labels to describe who we are at the core levels of our hearts. Some think of themselves as athletes or intellectuals. Others think of themselves as musicians, students, leaders, class clowns, and so on.

Disciples of Jesus set aside those labels and base their identities on Him. For example:

- **A disciple of Jesus is a child of God.** In the Bible we find these words: "Look at how great a love the Father has given us that we should be called God's children. And we are!" (1 John 3:1). We are God's children. He loves us as our perfect Father.

- **A disciple of Jesus is an alien in this world.** Disciples of Jesus are aliens, or outsiders, in their own cultures. Because of this identity, Jesus' disciples abstain from actions and activities that are contrary to Him. Peter, one of Jesus' original disciples, wrote these words: "Dear friends, I urge you as strangers and temporary residents to abstain from fleshly desires that war against you" (1 Peter 2:11).

- **A disciple of Jesus is an ambassador for Christ.** Another of Jesus' disciples recorded these words in the Bible: "Therefore, if anyone is in Christ, he is a new creation; old things have passed away, and look, new things have come. … Therefore, we are ambassadors for Christ, certain that God is appealing through us. We plead on Christ's behalf, 'Be reconciled to God'" (2 Corinthians 5:17,20). Ambassadors represent their king and country in a different culture for a specified period of time. Because we have been transformed by Jesus and are now His disciples and ambassadors, we represent Him to the world through our actions and by telling others about Him.

The journey you are about to take is one that will transform you more and more to be like Jesus. Enjoy! No one ever loved and cared for people more passionately than Jesus. No one was ever more sincere in His concern for others than Jesus. And no one ever gave more so that we could experience His love than did Jesus on the cross.

As you grow to be more like Jesus, you'll find that your relationships are stronger, you have more inner peace than ever before, and you look forward to the future as never before.

That's the blessing of living as a disciple of Jesus.

HOW TO USE THIS RESOURCE

Welcome to *The Way*. By exploring the journey of Jesus' earliest disciples, both new and established Christians will gain a better understanding of what it means to follow Christ. As you get started, consider the following guides and suggestions for making the most of this experience.

GROUP DISCUSSION

Because the process of discipleship always involves at least two people—the leader and the disciple—each session of *The Way* includes a practical plan for group engagement and discussion.

This plan includes the following steps:

- **Get Started.** The first section of the group material helps you ease into the discussion by starting on common ground. You'll begin by reflecting on the previous session and your recent experiences as a disciple. After spending time in prayer, you'll find a practical illustration to help you launch into the main topic of the current session.

- **The Story.** While using *Disciples Path*, you'll find opportunities to engage the Bible through both story and teaching. That's why the group time for each session features two main sections: **Know the Story** and **Unpack the Story. Know the Story** introduces a biblical text and includes follow-up questions for brief discussion. It's recommended that your group encounter the biblical text by reading it out loud. **Unpack the Story** includes practical teaching material and discussion questions—both designed to help you engage the truths contained in the biblical text. To make the most of your experience, use the provided material as a launching point for deeper conversation. As you read through the teaching material and engage the questions as a group, be thinking of how the truths you're exploring will impact your everyday life.

- **Engage.** The group portion of each session ends with an activity designed to help you practice the biblical principles introduced in Know the Story, which are fully explored in Unpack the Story. This part of the group time often appeals to different learning styles and will push you to engage the text at a personal level.

INDIVIDUAL DISCOVERY

Each session of *The Way* also includes content for individual use during the time between group gatherings. This content is divided into three categories:

⬆ **Worship:** features content for worship and devotion. These activities provide opportunities for you to connect with God in meaningful ways and deepen your relationship with Him.

➡ ⬅ **Personal study:** features content for personal study. These pages help you gain a deeper understanding of the truths and principles explored during the group discussion.

⬅ ➡ **Application:** features content for practical application. These suggestions help you take action based on the information you've learned as you grow in Christ.

Note: Aside from the reading plan, the content provided in the individual discovery portion of each session should be considered optional. You'll get the most out of your personal study by working with your group leader to create a personalized discipleship plan using the "Optional Activities" checklist included in each session.

ADDITIONAL SUGGESTIONS

- You'll be best prepared for each group discussion or mentoring conversation if you read the session material beforehand. A serious read will serve you most effectively, but skimming the Get Started and The Story sections will also be helpful if time is limited.

- The deeper you're willing to engage in the group discussions and individual discovery each session, the more you'll benefit from those experiences. Don't hold back, and don't be afraid to ask questions whenever necessary.

- As you explore the Engage portion of each session, you'll have the chance to practice different activities and spiritual disciplines. Take advantage of the chance to observe others during the group time—and to ask questions—so that you'll be prepared to incorporate these activities into your private spiritual life as well.

- Visit *Lifeway.com/DisciplesPath* for a free PDF download that includes leader helps for *The Way* and additional resources for disciple-makers.

SESSION 1
DEFINING A DISCIPLE

To be a disciple of Jesus is to participate in God's redemptive mission for the world.

REFLECT

Welcome to *The Way*. The goal of this resource is to help you explore the process of growing and maturing as a disciple of Jesus. Throughout the following sessions, we'll examine the journey of Jesus' own disciples as we study different passages from the Gospels. In this session, we'll begin by gaining a better understanding of what a disciple is and what it means to live each day as a disciple of Christ.

Use the following questions to begin the session with discussion.

What are some words our culture uses to describe those who choose to live for Jesus?

What are some words that describe your own experiences while living for Jesus?

In what ways would you most like to grow and mature in your efforts to follow Jesus?

PRAY

Take a break from your discussion to approach God in prayer. Use the following guidelines as you connect with Him:

- Thank God for the opportunity to join with other followers of Christ in order to gain a better understanding of what it means to live as a disciple.

- Praise God for the ways He has worked in your life.

- Ask for wisdom for all present as you engage God's Word.

INTRODUCTION

The English language has a lot of quirks. There are many rules and principles that are supposed to keep things separated and in order. Yet many times those rules and principles overlap in strange ways—even contradicting at times.

For example, did you know there are hundreds of English words that can be used as both a noun and a verb? Think of a farmer milking a cow. The word *milk* acts as a verb in such situations; to "milk" a cow is an action that involves specific steps. But what do you get after the cow has been milked? You get milk, of course—*milk* as a noun. The same word goes in two separate directions.

Other words follow the same pattern. You might *smell* (verb) something wonderful in your kitchen and recognize it as the *smell* (noun) of baking bread. You can use a *hammer* (noun) to *hammer* (verb) nails into a board. Strange as it may sound, it's entirely possible to chant a chant, broadcast a broadcast, and drink a drink.

Disciple is another word that can go in two directions at once. Those who have experienced salvation live and breathe each day as disciples of Jesus Christ. In this way, the word *disciple* defines who we are as Christians. At the same time, the term also defines much of what we do as Christians. As followers of Jesus, we're called to disciple less-mature Christians by helping them grow in their relationships with Christ—even as we are discipled by others.

This process is called "discipleship," and it's one of the primary goals of this resource. As you engage the pages to come, you'll learn what it means to find your identity as a disciple of Jesus. You'll also learn (and experience) the benefits of discipleship in the context of deeper relationships with other Christians.

How would you summarize what it means to be a disciple of Jesus Christ?

What questions do you have about the meaning and process of discipleship?

KNOW THE STORY

John the Baptist was a man with a mission. He had been charged by God to prepare the way for the Messiah—for Jesus. The following story highlights Jesus' mission for the world. It also helps us gain a sense of our place in that mission as disciples of Christ.

²⁹ The next day John saw Jesus coming toward him and said, "Here is the Lamb of God, who takes away the sin of the world! ³⁰ This is the One I told you about: 'After me comes a man who has surpassed me, because He existed before me.' ³¹ I didn't know Him, but I came baptizing with water so He might be revealed to Israel."

³² And John testified, "I watched the Spirit descending from heaven like a dove, and He rested on Him. ³³ I didn't know Him, but He who sent me to baptize with water told me, 'The One you see the Spirit descending and resting on—He is the One who baptizes with the Holy Spirit.' ³⁴ I have seen and testified that He is the Son of God!"

³⁵ Again the next day, John was standing with two of his disciples. ³⁶ When he saw Jesus passing by, he said, "Look! The Lamb of God!" ³⁷ The two disciples heard him say this and followed Jesus. ³⁸ When Jesus turned and noticed them following Him, He asked them, "What are you looking for?" They said to Him, "Rabbi" (which means "Teacher"), "where are You staying?" ³⁹ "Come and you'll see," He replied. So they went and saw where He was staying, and they stayed with Him that day. It was about 10 in the morning.

⁴⁰ Andrew, Simon Peter's brother, was one of the two who heard John and followed Him. ⁴¹ He first found his own brother Simon and told him, "We have found the Messiah!" (which means "Anointed One"), ⁴² and he brought Simon to Jesus.
JOHN 1:29-42

What do these verses teach us about Jesus?

UNPACK THE STORY
JESUS HAS A MISSION FOR THE WORLD

We're exploring the question: *what does it mean to be a disciple of Jesus?* Interestingly, the best way to answer that question is to focus not on the concept of a "disciple," but on the identity of Jesus. In order to understand what it means to live as followers of Jesus, we must first have a proper view of Jesus Himself.

What are some different ways people define Jesus today?

How would you express or explain who Jesus is?

John the Baptist offered several identifying factors for Jesus. For example, John claimed that Jesus existed before him, even though John was older than Jesus by several months. (See Luke 1.) More importantly, John identified Jesus as "the Lamb of God," "the Son of God," and "the One who baptizes with the Holy Spirit."

All of these factors point to a vital truth: Jesus is more than a regular person. In fact, Jesus is God in human flesh. One of the foundational concepts of Christianity is the doctrine of the incarnation, which states that Jesus is both fully God and fully human. Jesus' time on earth involved the fullness of God interacting with humanity and all of creation both physically and historically.

Jesus didn't come to earth for a vacation, but He had a purpose. He had a mission. And it was this mission John the Baptist referenced when he saw Jesus for the first time: "Here is the Lamb of God, who takes away the sin of the world!" (v. 29).

The world has been broken and corrupted by sin. We, as individuals, are broken and corrupted by sin. But Jesus came to fix the problem of sin. His death and resurrection opened the door for redemption—they allow us to experience forgiveness for our sins and live in a restored (or redeemed) relationship with God. This is the gospel.

How have you seen Jesus fix the problem of sin in your own life or in the life of someone you know?

To live as disciples of Jesus, we must first understand His redemptive mission for the world.

DISCIPLES PARTICIPATE IN JESUS' MISSION FOR THE WORLD

As with most things, however, it's not enough for us to simply *understand* Jesus' redemptive mission for the world. We must go further. We must take action. Indeed, to be a disciple of Jesus is to *participate* in His mission and purpose for the world.

Notice from our Scripture focus that John the Baptist wasn't content with recognizing Jesus as "the Lamb of God." John publicly proclaimed the truth about Jesus on multiple occasions. He took action in order to participate in Jesus' mission and purpose. And his participation paid off—men who had been following John were rightly convinced to follow Jesus, instead. (See vv. 37-39.)

In a similar way, verse 40 shows how Andrew—one of the two men who had been following John—participated in Jesus' mission by sharing the good news with his brother, Simon. Andrew's efforts went beyond words. He brought Simon to Jesus so that his brother could experience the truth for himself.

How would you describe your experiences of talking with others about Jesus?

What are some other ways we can participate in Jesus' mission for the world?

As you read through Scripture—and as you work through the pages of this resource—you'll notice that Jesus' disciples rarely engage His mission as individuals. Instead, followers of Christ typically work together in relationship with one another as they seek to advance His redemptive mission in the world.

That was certainly Jesus' preference during His public ministry. He didn't recruit converts and then send them out to do His work in isolation. Instead, He gathered disciples to Himself so they could follow Him as a community—even as a family.

When have you worked with a group or on a team to engage Jesus' mission for the world? What are the advantages of this?

ENGAGE

Following Jesus is not an individual activity, nor is it something that can be accomplished in isolation—not for long. Instead, living as a disciple of Christ means living within a community of Christians. That community extends around the world and throughout time to include the church in all ages and all locations. On a more practical level, however, your local community includes the fellow disciples you connect with, worship with, and serve with each week.

Take a few minutes to practice living as a community of disciples in the following two ways:

1. Pray with one another. Spend several minutes praying together as a group. Talk openly about the major events in your life, including both difficulties and triumphs. Then take turns praying for one another, specifically and intentionally.

2. Connect with one another. Plan a time to meet socially as a group and do something fun, preferably before the next group meeting. Meet at a park, go to a ball game, watch a movie—anything that moves you forward together in community.

PRAYER REQUESTS:

....

....

....

....

....

....

....

....

....

....

....

....

In addition to studying God's Word, work with your group leader to create a plan for personal study, worship, and application between now and the next session. Select from the following optional activities to match your personal preferences and available time.

⬆ Worship

☑ Read your Bible. Complete the reading plan on page 16.

☐ Spend time with God by reading the devotional and answering the questions on page 17.

☐ Connect with God each day through prayer.

➡ ⬅ Personal Study

☐ Read and interact with "Jesus Has a Mission for the World" on page 18.

☐ Read and interact with "Disciples Participate in Jesus' Mission" on page 20.

⬅ ➡ Application

☐ Make the most of your experiences at church this weekend. Take advantage of opportunities to engage others in a more meaningful way.

☐ Memorize John 1:29: "The next day John saw Jesus coming toward him and said, 'Here is the Lamb of God, who takes away the sin of the world!'"

☐ When you have an opportunity to participate in Jesus' mission this week, invite a friend to join you.

☐ Start a journal to record the different ways you participate in Jesus' mission for the world each day. This is a great way to remind yourself of why Jesus came and your role in His mission.

☐ Other:

↑ WORSHIP

READING PLAN

Read through the following passages this week. Use the space provided to record your thoughts and responses.

Day 1
Luke 14:25-35

Day 2
John 15:1-18

Day 3
John 17:6-19

Day 4
John 21:15-23

Day 5
Ephesians 4:17-32

Day 6
2 Timothy 2:1-13

Day 7
2 Timothy 2:14-26

TO SERVE AND TO GIVE

As you'd expect, Jesus' earliest disciples had a lot of learning to do about what it meant to follow Him. For example, they spent much of their time in a strange kind of sibling rivalry—they pushed and jockeyed with one another in order to see who would become the greatest in Jesus' kingdom. The disciples knew Jesus was special, and they understood Him to be both majestic and powerful. Therefore, each wanted to position himself to receive the largest portion of reflected majesty and power once Jesus declared Himself to the world as King.

Of course, none of that was in Jesus' plans. And He let them know it:

> [42] Jesus called them over and said to them, "You know that those who are regarded as rulers of the Gentiles dominate them, and their men of high positions exercise power over them. [43] But it must not be like that among you. On the contrary, whoever wants to become great among you must be your servant, [44] and whoever wants to be first among you must be a slave to all. [45] For even the Son of Man did not come to be served, but to serve, and to give His life—a ransom for many."
> **MARK 10:42-45**

We, too, must guard against pride and ambition as we seek to follow Jesus—mainly because such attitudes will damage our relationship with Him. Use the following questions to assess your heart.

What causes you to feel jealous of or competitive with other Christians?

In what situations do you see yourself as superior to other people? Why?

How do you feel when you do something for the benefit of others, not just yourself?

Following Jesus isn't about notoriety and big rewards—not in this life, anyway. Instead, those who choose to live as disciples of Christ must constantly give of themselves in order to serve others, as He did.

JESUS HAS A MISSION FOR THE WORLD

What does it mean to be a disciple of Jesus? At the core, it means to join with other disciples in order to participate in His broader mission for the world. To that end, we've already seen that Jesus' mission centers on His role as "the One who takes away the sin of the world" (John 1:29). But let's dig a little deeper into that mission—and into the identify of Jesus Himself—in order to better understand what's expected of us as disciples.

John the Baptist provides an interesting character study for these themes. While he spent his life preparing the way for the Messiah, he didn't encounter Jesus until the end of his ministry. Yet we can learn much from John when it comes to understanding how we are to live in light of who Jesus is and His mission for the world.

Look at the following passage, for example:

> ¹⁵ Now the people were waiting expectantly, and all of them were debating in their minds whether John might be the Messiah. ¹⁶ John answered them all, "I baptize you with water, but One is coming who is more powerful than I. I am not worthy to untie the strap of His sandals. He will baptize you with the Holy Spirit and fire. ¹⁷ His winnowing shovel is in His hand to clear His threshing floor and gather the wheat into His barn, but the chaff He will burn up with a fire that never goes out."
> LUKE 3:15-17

What can we learn about John the Baptist from these verses?

What can we learn about Jesus from these verses?

The people of John's day were looking for the Messiah, a specific term for the Savior of the world prophesied throughout the Old Testament. John knew the Messiah would be Someone greater than himself—Someone with the power to both save people for eternity ("gather the wheat into His barn") and pronounce judgment for sin ("the chaff He will burn up").

In addition, John understood that the Messiah would grant people access to God's Spirit. John baptized people with water as a symbol. The Messiah would baptize "with the Holy Spirit and fire."

All of this is important because it helps us understand that Jesus' mission for the world is directly connected to His divine authority and divine identity. The reason Jesus can fix the brokenness of the world is because He created the world. The reason Jesus can provide forgiveness for sin is because He is God and therefore He is totally untouched by sin. For these reasons and more, we can feel confident as participants in Jesus' mission.

In order to live as disciples of Jesus, we must first fully embrace His identity as God. Thankfully, Jesus made His identity clear throughout the Scriptures, including here:

> ^{27} My sheep hear My voice, I know them, and they follow Me. ^{28} I give them eternal life, and they will never perish—ever! No one will snatch them out of My hand. ^{29} My Father, who has given them to Me, is greater than all. No one is able to snatch them out of the Father's hand. ^{30} The Father and I are one.
> JOHN 10:27-30

How did you come to the conclusion that Jesus is God?

In a similar way, Jesus wasn't silent about the nature of His mission for the world. He spoke often of His purpose and His goals as Savior.

Read the following passages of Scripture. How do they help you understand Jesus' mission for the world?

Mark 10:42-45

Luke 4:16-21

John 17:1-5

Living as a disciple of Jesus means embracing His identity and His mission for the world. Be sure you've taken that crucial step as you consider what it means to follow Him each day.

DISCIPLES PARTICIPATE IN JESUS' MISSION

In order to live as disciples of Jesus, we must fully embrace His mission as the divine Savior of the world. But that's just the first step. In addition to understanding and embracing Jesus' mission for the world, we must also participate in that mission. We need to get involved.

But what does that mean on a practical level? How do we actually go about joining Jesus in His redemptive purpose for the world? We'll spend the remainder of this resource exploring answers to those questions. Specifically, we'll focus on four ways Jesus empowers those who follow Him:

1. Jesus calls His disciples.
2. Jesus teaches His disciples.
3. Jesus equips His disciples.
4. Jesus sends His disciples.

Which item from this list are you most interested in exploring? Why?

Before we move forward, however, let's look at two important truths that will help us gain a deeper understanding of what it means to participate in Jesus' mission for the world. First, our involvement in Jesus' mission goes beyond "participation" in the normal sense of that word. We don't participate with Jesus in the same way we participate in community service projects or helping out around the house— we don't just "pitch in" with Jesus' mission whenever we have the time.

No, to follow Jesus means to give up our lives in service to Him. Jesus Himself made that clear:

> ²³ Then He said to them all, "If anyone wants to come with Me, he must deny himself, take up his cross daily, and follow Me. ²⁴ For whoever wants to save his life will lose it, but whoever loses his life because of Me will save it.
> LUKE 9:23-24

What's your initial reaction to Jesus' instructions here?

Jesus wasn't necessarily talking about physically dying for His mission—although many of His followers have done so over the centuries. Instead, Jesus wanted us to understand that joining His purpose for the world means giving over control of our lives to Him. Following Jesus means we not only recognize Him as Savior, but also submit to Him as Master, Lord, and King.

In what ways have you already submitted yourself to Jesus?

What steps can you take in the coming weeks to continue releasing control of your life over to Him?

Second, we need to understand that our involvement in Jesus' mission depends on His strength and resources rather than our own. It's easy for Christians to get the wrong idea on this subject—it's easy for us to feel like the world is on our shoulders and all of God's plans will collapse if we don't pray harder, worship longer, read the Bible more frequently, and evangelize until we drop.

Thankfully, Jesus again made things clear in His Word:

> "I am the vine; you are the branches. The one who remains in Me and I in him produces much fruit, because you can do nothing without Me."
> JOHN 15:5

How have you benefited from Jesus' presence and power in your life?

What kinds of fruit do you hope will be produced in your life as a disciple of Jesus?

As a disciple of Jesus, you will participate in His mission when you submit control of your life to Him and actively rely on His resources to work through you.

SESSION 2
JESUS CALLS HIS DISCIPLES

Christ meets us where we are and transforms us as we follow Him.

REFLECT

We saw in the previous session that Jesus has a specific mission for the world: to redeem the world and those of us who dwell in it from the corruption of sin. We also saw that living as a disciple of Jesus means not only understanding Jesus' redemptive purpose for the world, but embracing the opportunity to participate in that mission as we live each day.

As you prepare to explore how Jesus calls His disciples, take a moment to reflect on your experiences in recent days.

Which of the assignments did you explore this week? How did it go?

What did you learn or experience while reading the Bible?

What questions would you like to ask before we move forward?

PRAY

Begin this session by connecting with God through prayer. Use the following guidelines as you speak with Him together:

- Praise God for giving you the opportunity to participate in His mission for the world.

- Express gratitude and thanks for the ways in which Jesus has invited you to be on mission with Him. Ask for clarity as you think through your earliest encounters with Him.

- Ask for wisdom to engage the Bible as you explore what it means to be "called" as a disciple of Christ.

INTRODUCTION

"I want YOU!"

Most Americans are familiar with the famous recruitment poster of Uncle Sam—dressed in a blue suit, red tie, and white-starred hat—pointing directly at the viewer. His face is stern and serious. His posture is confident, and his white hair offers an air of both authority and experience. The full text reads, "I want YOU for the U.S. Army."

What many Americans don't know is that the image for the poster was first created as a magazine cover for the July 6 issue of *Leslie's Weekly* in 1916 with the title, "What Are You Doing for Preparedness?" The image was adapted into the now-famous military poster and printed more than 4 million times between 1917 and 1918 as a recruitment tool during World War I. Because of its success, the poster was used again decades later when America entered World War II.

James Montgomery Flagg, the artist who originally created the image, later declared it to be "the most famous poster in the world."

One reason the poster has maintained its popularity is because it reminds us of the deeper connection that exists between us and our nation. We are not a loose collection of individuals running around and doing our own thing—though it may seem that way at times. We are Americans. In times of war or crisis, the poster is a call to action encouraging us not only to remember our national identity, but also to participate in defending the key ideas and principles that define our way of life.

When have you been excited to join a group or a cause?

What is a recruitment slogan or call-to-action you've found compelling?

As we'll see in this session, Jesus had different ways of recruiting His disciples during His public ministry on earth—but He did recruit them. He actively searched for followers and called them to join Him in His mission for the world.

Jesus still recruits His disciples today. In fact, the first step in living as a disciple of Christ is to answer His call.

KNOW THE STORY

In the early days of His public ministry, Jesus intentionally gathered a number of disciples around Him. As was the custom of rabbis in those days, Jesus intended for these young men to follow Him during His travels in order to both learn from Him and contribute to His ministry.

The following story shows how Jesus called two of those first disciples.

[43] The next day He decided to leave for Galilee. Jesus found Philip and told him, "Follow Me!" [44] Now Philip was from Bethsaida, the hometown of Andrew and Peter. [45] Philip found Nathanael and told him, "We have found the One Moses wrote about in the Law (and so did the prophets): Jesus the son of Joseph, from Nazareth!" [46] "Can anything good come out of Nazareth?" Nathanael asked him. "Come and see," Philip answered.

[47] Then Jesus saw Nathanael coming toward Him and said about him, "Here is a true Israelite; no deceit is in him." [48] "How do you know me?" Nathanael asked. "Before Philip called you, when you were under the fig tree, I saw you," Jesus answered.

[49] "Rabbi," Nathanael replied, "You are the Son of God! You are the King of Israel!"

[50] Jesus responded to him, "Do you believe only because I told you I saw you under the fig tree? You will see greater things than this." [51] Then He said, "I assure you: You will see heaven opened and the angels of God ascending and descending on the Son of Man."
JOHN 1:43-51

What do these verses teach us about following Jesus?

How would you summarize the process through which Nathanael became a disciple?

UNPACK THE STORY
DISCIPLES HAVE AN ENCOUNTER WITH JESUS

The first step in becoming a disciple of Jesus is encountering Him in a deep and meaningful way. Nobody inherits a relationship with Jesus from their parents. No one earns their status as a disciple by attending church, doing good things, or avoiding bad things.

We become disciples of Christ when we experience Him in a way that changes our lives.

How has your life been changed by an encounter with Jesus?

Looking at John 1:43-51, it's interesting that Philip and Nathanael encountered Jesus in different ways. Philip received a direct call from Jesus. The Savior sought him out specifically and said: "Follow me." Nathaniel, on the other hand, took a little more seasoning. He resisted Philip's attempts at evangelism, scoffing at the notion that the Messiah—the One prophesied in the Scriptures as the Savior of God's people—could come from an insignificant town like Nazareth. Even when he met Jesus, Nathanael challenged His assessment of his own character, asking, "How do you know me?"

Fortunately for Nathanael, he wasn't stubborn to the point of unbelief. When Jesus revealed Himself in a supernatural way, Nathanael responded by submitting himself before the Savior in worship and praise. "You are the Son of God!" he said, acknowledging that Jesus was indeed the Messiah. "You are the King of Israel!"

All of this tells us there's no template for receiving the call to follow Jesus. There are no magic words you *have* to say and no amount of steps you *must* follow in order to officially be considered a Christian. Instead, followers of Jesus are simply those who respond to His call.

What have you heard or been taught about the process of salvation?

What have you heard or been taught about what happens after salvation?

DISCIPLES ARE TRANSFORMED BY JESUS

We noted earlier that the first step in becoming a disciple of Jesus is encountering Him in a way that changes our lives. That was certainly the case with both Philip and Nathanael.

For example, notice that Philip responded to his encounter with Jesus by immediately seeking out the people he cared about and telling them about Jesus. He wanted them to have a similar encounter, so he proclaimed the good news without shame or hesitation. He was transformed into an evangelist— seemingly in an instant.

Don't miss that. Too often Christians feel like they need to become "mature" before they can start sharing the gospel message. Too many disciples remain silent about their encounters with Jesus because they don't want to be seen as weird, or they don't want to impose on the time and beliefs of others.

The truth is that when we experience something that changes our lives for the better, we almost can't stop sharing the news. That's our natural reaction when we encounter something (or Someone) that brings us joy.

What emotions do you experience at the thought of sharing the gospel with those you care about?

Nathanael was also changed by his encounter with Jesus. When he was first told about Jesus, he was skeptical and a little sarcastic. But after meeting Jesus face-to-face, he responded with genuine worship. His behavior changed after responding to Jesus' call.

Of course, this was just the beginning of their spiritual transformation. Both Philip and Nathanael walked with Jesus for years before His death and resurrection. Afterward, they served faithfully in the early church and, according to church tradition, were eventually martyred for their faith in Christ. Throughout their lives, they continued to grow and mature as disciples of Jesus. The same should be true of us.

How is your life different than it was before you followed Christ?

ENGAGE

Talking through your earliest encounters with Jesus is a great way to share the gospel message with those who need to hear it. You don't need a fancy testimony or a miniature sermon—simply share what you've experienced and how you've changed as a result.

Use the space below to outline or sketch your earliest encounters with Jesus and how those experiences have changed your life. After a few minutes, practice sharing your story with someone else.

Your First Encounters with Jesus

How You've Changed

PRAYER REQUESTS:

....

....

....

....

....

In addition to studying God's Word, work with your group leader to create a plan for personal study, worship, and application between now and the next session. Select from the following optional activities to match your personal preferences and available time.

⬆ Worship

☑ Read your Bible. Complete the reading plan on page 30.

☐ Spend time with God by reading the devotion and answering the questions on page 31.

☐ Connect with God each day through prayer.

➡ ⬅ Personal Study

☐ Read and interact with "Disciples Have an Encounter with Jesus" on page 32.

☐ Read and interact with "Disciples Are Transformed by Jesus" on page 34.

⬅ ➡ Application

☐ Look for an opportunity to share your testimony this week. When you feel the time is right to share the gospel with someone in your life, talk openly about your experiences as a disciple of Jesus.

☐ Seek a fresh encounter with Jesus. It's easy to fall into a routine as a follower of Jesus. Therefore, make an effort to connect with Christ in a new or refreshing way.

☐ Memorize Mark 2:17: "When Jesus heard this, He told them, 'Those who are well don't need a doctor, but the sick do need one. I didn't come to call the righteous, but sinners.'"

☐ Journal about your earliest encounters with Jesus. Write down what you experienced when you first decided to follow Christ and how your life has changed since.

☐ Other:

WORSHIP

READING PLAN

Read through the following passages this week. Use the space provided to record your thoughts and responses.

Day 1
Matthew 5:1-16

Day 2
Luke 5:1-11

Day 3
Romans 5:1-21

Day 4
Romans 12:1-21

Day 5
Ephesians 4:17-32

Day 6
Colossians 3:1-17

Day 7
Revelation 21:1-27

JESUS' PRAYER

John 17 is an interesting chapter within the Gospels. The whole chapter is a long prayer recited by Jesus near the end of the Last Supper with His disciples. Jesus began by praying for Himself, asking that the Father would glorify Him even as He sought to glorify the Father by doing the work He had been called to do. Next, Jesus spent several verses praying for the disciples who were with Him.

Can you imagine what it would be like for Jesus to pray for you, specifically? Actually, that happened! After praying for the disciples physically present with Him at the time, Jesus prayed for all His disciples that would come later—including you.

Here's the first part of that prayer:

> ²⁰ I pray not only for these,
> but also for those who believe in Me
> through their message.
> ²¹ May they all be one,
> as You, Father, are in Me and I am in You.
> May they also be one in Us,
> so the world may believe You sent Me.
> **JOHN 17:20-21**

How does it make you feel to know that Jesus prayed for you before His sacrifice on the cross?

Read Jesus' entire prayer in John 17:20-26. What strikes you as most interesting in these verses? Why?

Spend a few moments echoing Jesus by praying through these verses, then listen for God to speak. How is He speaking to your heart?

DISCIPLES HAVE AN ENCOUNTER WITH JESUS

Philip and Nathanael were personally called by Jesus to follow Him. The same is true of many others during Jesus' life, including men like Peter, James, John, and Matthew (Matt. 10:2-4)—and also women such as Mary Magdalene, Joanna, and Susanna (Luke 8:1-3). These individuals and many more served and supported Jesus during His ministry on earth.

What's interesting is that Jesus continued to call people to Himself even after His earthly ministry was over—even after His death, resurrection, and ascension had been accomplished. For example, Jesus personally and specifically reached out to a Pharisee named Saul of Tarshish:

> [1] Meanwhile, Saul was still breathing threats and murder against the disciples of the Lord. He went to the high priest [2] and requested letters from him to the synagogues in Damascus, so that if he found any men or women who belonged to the Way, he might bring them as prisoners to Jerusalem. [3] As he traveled and was nearing Damascus, a light from heaven suddenly flashed around him. [4] Falling to the ground, he heard a voice saying to him, "Saul, Saul, why are you persecuting Me?"
>
> [5] "Who are You, Lord?" he said.
>
> "I am Jesus, the One you are persecuting," He replied. [6] "But get up and go into the city, and you will be told what you must do."
> **ACTS 9:1-6**

Saul had been fully dedicated to his direction in life, which happened to involve "breathing threats and murder against the disciples of the Lord." When he encountered Jesus, however, and responded to Jesus' call—everything changed. Saul changed. He turned completely away from his old way of life and started down the path of following Christ. Today, we know Saul by his other name: the apostle Paul.

Paul's story is important because it reminds us of the need for repentance as we respond to Jesus' call.

What ideas or images come to mind when you hear the word "repent"?

To repent is to turn away from something or change your mind. And that's what Jesus calls us to do—He wants us to turn away from our old lives and old directions and to follow Him, instead. In fact, according to the Gospel of Matthew, repentance was the primary theme of Jesus' early ministry:

> From then on Jesus began to preach, "Repent, because the kingdom of heaven has come near!"
> **MATTHEW 4:17**

> [14] After John was arrested, Jesus went to Galilee, preaching the good news of God: [15] "The time is fulfilled, and the kingdom of God has come near. Repent and believe in the good news!"
> **MARK 1:14-15**

What part did repentance play in your decision to follow Jesus?

Repentance is a necessary step in answering Jesus' call. However, it's not a step you only take once. We continue to wander away from God and from His mission for the world even after we choose to follow Him.

Therefore, to be a disciple of Jesus is to live a life of repentance in which we regularly turn away from our sin and choose once again to answer His call.

In what areas of life do you currently need to repent of your sin and return to Jesus?

What steps can you take to make sure repentance is a regular part of your spiritual life?

DISCIPLES ARE TRANSFORMED BY JESUS

It's true that the apostle Paul made a conscious decision to repent after encountering Jesus on the road to Damascus. He moved from completely opposing the cause of Christ—from persecuting and even murdering Jesus' disciples—to investing his resources in the advancement of that cause. He completely changed the trajectory of his life.

Yet it's also true that Paul didn't make such a drastic turn completely on his own. He was able to change the course of his life because *he* had been changed. Paul was transformed during his encounter with Jesus—he became someone different than he had been.

Today we refer to this phenomenon as spiritual transformation. Paul himself described it best during one of his letters to the early church:

> Therefore, if anyone is in Christ, he is a new creation; old things have passed away, and look, new things have come.
> **2 CORINTHIANS 5:17**

What are some "old things" that have passed away in your life?

What "new things" have you experienced since encountering Jesus?

The type of transformation we experience immediately after encountering Jesus is known as justification. This is a legal term that highlights the guilt we all carry because of our sin. The good news of the gospel is that when we respond to God's call, we experience forgiveness from our sins in a way that changes our legal standing before God—we become justified in God's eyes because we are covered with the righteousness of Jesus. Paul explains:

> [9] Much more then, since we have now been declared righteous by His blood, we will be saved through Him from wrath. [10] For if, while we were enemies, we were reconciled to God through the death of His Son, then how much more, having been reconciled, will we be saved by His life!
> **ROMANS 5:9-10**

Read the following Scripture passages and record how they contribute to your understanding of justification.

Hebrews 9:19-22

Romans 5:6-9

Galatians 2:15-16

While justification describes the spiritual transformation we experience immediately upon encountering Jesus and choosing to follow Him, that's not the end. In fact, to follow Jesus is to continually be transformed so that we become more and more like Him as we continue to follow Him. This ongoing transformation brings us closer and closer to the people God originally designed us to be.

This process is known as sanctification. To sanctify something means to set it apart. As disciples, we are set apart by and for God. We are in the process of being made more like God's Son. Once again, Paul helps us understand:

> We all, with unveiled faces, are looking as in a mirror at the glory of the Lord and are being transformed into the same image from glory to glory; this is from the Lord who is the Spirit.
> **2 CORINTHIANS 3:18**

Do you feel you've regularly experienced spiritual transformation as a follower of Jesus? Explain.

What obstacles are currently holding you back from becoming the person God has set you apart to be?

SESSION 3
JESUS TEACHES HIS DISCIPLES

Disciples are called to learn about
Jesus and learn from Jesus.

REFLECT

In the previous session, we explored some of the different ways in which Jesus called His earliest disciples. We also continued to broaden our understanding of what it means to live as a disciple of Jesus by noting that all disciples have an encounter with Jesus that begins a process of spiritual transformation—a process that will continue to change us throughout our lives into the people we were originally created to be.

As you prepare to explore how Jesus teaches His disciples, take a moment to reflect on your experiences in recent days.

Which of the assignments did you explore this week? How did it go?

What did you learn or experience while reading the Bible?

What questions would you like to ask before we move forward?

PRAY

Begin this session by connecting with God through prayer. Use the following guidelines as you speak with Him together:

- Thank God for the ways He has called you into His kingdom, and for His continued work of spiritual transformation in your life.

- Ask for God to speak clearly to your heart through His Word. Ask for wisdom to understand the truths you will encounter as you engage the Bible.

- Submit to God as your Teacher and commit to applying what you learn throughout this study.

INTRODUCTION

When you hear the word *counterfeit*, what's the first thing that pops into your head? It's money, right? Criminals produce counterfeit money and try to pass it off as genuine bills, seeking to trick merchants into accepting the fake currency.

Because counterfeit money is a real threat, cashiers and other people who deal regularly with cash need to learn how to tell the difference between what's real and what's counterfeit. Bank tellers, specifically, are trained to detect counterfeit bills so that their bank isn't left in the lurch with fraudulent money.

The way bank tellers are trained to spot counterfeits is interesting. They don't learn about methods for counterfeiting money. They don't get profiles on the people who produce counterfeit currency. They don't even spend time studying fake $100 bills. Instead, bank employees learn to spot counterfeit currency *by intensely studying the real thing*. They train their eyes and their senses by watching, smelling, feeling, and continually interacting with real money in order to spot fake money whenever it comes along.

The same is true for discipleship. If we want to know what a disciple should look like—what they should believe and do—we need to know the One we're called to follow.

The scary thing about counterfeits is that they look nearly identical to the real thing. On the surface, there appears to be no difference. Why is that scary? Because we could easily find ourselves going through the motions as disciples of Jesus, yet be false at the core. Many of the activities of a disciple can be practiced without integrity, and yet still appear to the world as authentic.

What are some common actions of Jesus' disciples that are easy to counterfeit?

Why is hypocrisy dangerous in God's kingdom?

It's time to study the real thing. In this session, we'll focus on Jesus as our Teacher. We'll seek to learn from Him—and learn about Him—as we explore our responsibilities in the process of moving forward as disciples of Christ.

KNOW THE STORY

Jesus' words in Matthew 5–7 are known today as the Sermon on the Mount. This is no doubt the most famous sermon ever preached, and it was delivered by the greatest Teacher who ever lived—therefore, it's worthy of our attention. But as we explore Jesus' sermon, let's focus on two key passages that are often overlooked.

> [1] When He saw the crowds, He went up on the mountain, and after He sat down, His disciples came to Him. [2] Then He began to teach them, saying:
> **MATTHEW 5:1-2**

> [24] "Everyone who hears these words of Mine and acts on them will be like a sensible man who built his house on the rock. [25] The rain fell, the rivers rose, and the winds blew and pounded that house. Yet it didn't collapse, because its foundation was on the rock. [26] But everyone who hears these words of Mine and doesn't act on them will be like a foolish man who built his house on the sand. [27] The rain fell, the rivers rose, the winds blew and pounded that house, and it collapsed. And its collapse was great!"
> [28] When Jesus had finished this sermon, the crowds were astonished at His teaching, [29] because He was teaching them like one who had authority, and not like their scribes.
> **MATTHEW 7:24-29**

When have you been amazed at a teacher's knowledge of a particular subject? How did his or her expertise make the lesson easier for you to understand?

What lesson was Jesus teaching in this passage?

Both of these passages help us grasp the necessity of learning from Jesus—and of taking action to obey what we learn—as we follow Him.

UNPACK THE STORY
DISCIPLES ADOPT A POSTURE TO LEARN

One of the hallmarks of Jesus' sermon was how He regularly turned common wisdom on its head in order to show us what a true disciple looks like. Jesus kept repeating the phrase "You have heard that it was said" before referencing interpretations of the Old Testament law or cultural norms. Then He would ratchet up the tension by saying, "But I tell you ..."

Again and again, Jesus called His disciples to a higher level of obedience. He pushed them to shape the culture around them rather than just follow what everyone else was doing.

> ***Read Matthew 5:1-12. Which of Jesus' statements do you find most countercultural? Why?***

As wonderful as it is to read Jesus' teaching, don't miss those first two verses:

> ¹ When He saw the crowds, He went up on the mountain, and after He sat down, His disciples came to Him. ² Then He began to teach them, saying:
> MATTHEW 5:1-2

Notice that not everyone heard Jesus' teaching. Not everyone followed Him up the mountain. But His disciples did. They had already abandoned much of their "normal" lives in order to travel with Jesus. And now they trekked up the side of a mountain to sit at His feet. Jesus' disciples placed themselves in a posture to learn. Therefore, they were blessed by His teaching.

> ***In what settings or situations do you most often hear from Jesus in a meaningful way?***
>
> ***How can you intentionally place yourself in a posture to learn from Jesus this week?***

Adopting a posture to learn from Jesus is a necessary step for His disciples. But it's not the final step in the process.

DISCIPLES OBEY WHAT THEY LEARN

When you think about it, there's a big difference between students and disciples. Both groups are interested in learning from a teacher. However, students learn for the sake of information; they learn in order to pass a test or achieve a degree. Disciples, on the other hand, learn for the sake of obedience. They learn in order to take action.

That's why Jesus regularly warned people to be conscious of their fruit. For example, look at what He said earlier in Matthew 7:

> 15 "Beware of false prophets who come to you in sheep's clothing but inwardly are ravaging wolves. 16 You'll recognize them by their fruit. Are grapes gathered from thornbushes or figs from thistles? 17 In the same way, every good tree produces good fruit, but a bad tree produces bad fruit.
> MATTHEW 7:15-17

Do your actions always match your beliefs? For example: Do you always follow your parents' advice when you know they are right?

When have you struggled to act on something you knew to be true?

The storms of life are difficult. Therefore, we need a firm foundation—we need something solid on which we can build our lives, weather the storms, and continue to participate in Jesus' mission for the world. Clearly, the teachings of Jesus offer the only sure foundation on which we can build. He is the Rock.

At the same time, Jesus' teachings only serve as a usable foundation *when they are acted upon.* Obedience is necessary if we want to avoid building on sand.

What are some key teachings of Jesus that all disciples should believe? (Skim through Matthew 5–7 for examples.)

What actions are required or implied by these teachings?

ENGAGE

Being part of a community is a great way to engage Jesus' teaching in a way that fosters both understanding and obedience. Joining with others to study God's Word is helpful when passages are especially deep or difficult to understand. And being in community offers a number of opportunities for accountability—it makes it more difficult for us to actively ignore what we know to be true.

For these reasons and more, work together to engage the following portion of Jesus' teaching:

[25] "This is why I tell you: Don't worry about your life, what you will eat or what you will drink; or about your body, what you will wear. Isn't life more than food and the body more than clothing? [26] Look at the birds of the sky: They don't sow or reap or gather into barns, yet your heavenly Father feeds them. Aren't you worth more than they? [27] Can any of you add a single cubit to his height by worrying? [28] And why do you worry about clothes? Learn how the wildflowers of the field grow: they don't labor or spin thread. [29] Yet I tell you that not even Solomon in all his splendor was adorned like one of these! [30] If that's how God clothes the grass of the field, which is here today and thrown into the furnace tomorrow, won't He do much more for you—you of little faith? [31] So don't worry, saying, 'What will we eat?' or 'What will we drink?' or 'What will we wear?' [32] For the idolaters eagerly seek all these things, and your heavenly Father knows that you need them. [33] But seek first the kingdom of God and His righteousness, and all these things will be provided for you. [34] Therefore don't worry about tomorrow, because tomorrow will worry about itself. Each day has enough trouble of its own.
MATTHEW 6:25-34

What are the key truths contained in this passage?

How can you apply these truths in your life this week?

PRAYER REQUESTS:

....

....

....

....

....

....

WEEKLY ACTIVITIES

In addition to studying God's Word, work with your group leader to create a plan for personal study, worship, and application between now and the next session. Select from the following optional activities to match your personal preferences and available time.

⬆ Worship

☑ Read your Bible. Complete the reading plan on page 44.

☐ Spend time with God by reading the devotion and answering the questions on page 45.

☐ Connect with God each day through prayer. Specifically, concentrate on smaller prayers throughout the day, asking that Jesus would help you remain in a posture to hear from Him and obey His teaching.

➡ ⬅ Personal Study

☐ Read and interact with "Disciples Adopt a Posture to Learn" on page 46.

☐ Read and interact with "Disciples Obey What They Learn" on page 48.

⬅ ➡ Application

☐ Read through the entire Sermon on the Mount (Matthew 5–7) this week. Consider reading it out loud as a way to increase your concentration on the text.

☐ Invite a friend or family member to study God's Word with you. Studying the Bible with others can help you understand and act upon what you learn.

☐ Memorize Matthew 7:24: "Everyone who hears these words of Mine and acts on them will be like a sensible man who built his house on the rock."

☐ To continue using your journal, write down the different ways you see the fruit of the Spirit in yourself and in the people around you. Be intentional to seek out examples and jot them down.

☐ Other:

 **WORSHIP**

READING PLAN

Read through the following passages this week. Use the space provided to record your thoughts and responses.

Day 1
Psalm 119:1-24

Day 2
Psalm 119:25-48

Day 3
Psalm 119:49-80

Day 4
Psalm 119:81-104

Day 5
Psalm 119:105-136

Day 6
Psalm 119:137-160

Day 7
Psalm 119:161-176

YOUR TRUE HEART

We've seen how important it is for our actions to match our beliefs—or what we claim to be our beliefs. The difficulty in achieving this is that we often deceive ourselves. We shy away from the truth about what we believe and what we do.

The prophet Jeremiah told us why:

> The heart is more deceitful than anything else,
> and incurable—who can understand it?
> **JEREMIAH 17:9**

How easily we let ourselves off the hook. We're quick to grant ourselves grace and mercy because we believe that deep down we really are good people with good intentions. We believe the best about ourselves and hope that everything will come out alright in the end. This is dangerous.

Fortunately, Jeremiah also offered the solution to our problem:

> I, Yahweh, examine the mind,
> I test the heart
> to give to each according to his way,
> according to what his actions deserve.
> **JEREMIAH 17:10**

Take a moment right now to pause and seek God's presence. Ask Him to "test" your true heart—to help you see more clearly how your actions match up with what you say you believe.

What has God revealed to you?

What do you need to do in response to that revelation?

DISCIPLES ADOPT A POSTURE TO LEARN

If you've ever had a conversation with someone who was also checking their phone, you know how frustrating it can be to have half a person's attention. Because, honestly, having half of someone's attention feels like having none of it. It's offensive, distracting, and unhelpful when a person is "there but not there." In the end, it costs everyone unnecessary extra time and attention to move forward.

Do you think God ever feels that way about us? Is it possible He says, "I'm willing to teach, but you're…"

- consumed by school.

- distracted by stress.

- pursuing pleasure.

- ignoring My Word.

The posture of our lives will tell God whether we really want to hear what He has to say. True disciples position themselves to hear from God. They structure their lives so that when God speaks, they're ready to listen and respond.

> *What habits or activities—even "good" ones—prevent you from positioning yourself to hear from God?*

Disciples of Jesus know it's not enough to simply "want" His truth. They go after it. They sacrifice for it. That's because receiving truth isn't a passive experience. To learn from Jesus is to actively bend your life around what matters most. In short, we don't grow as disciples by just listening to a sermon every week or even attending a Bible study.

Rather, disciples learn and grow by making small choices each day—sometimes each hour—to actively trust Jesus and listen for His voice.

> *How satisfied are you with your current efforts to learn from Jesus?*

1	2	3	4	5	6	7	8	9	10

Not satisfied   Very satisfied

In Matthew 5, we saw Jesus' disciples trek up a mountain in order to hear His teaching in what we now call the Sermon on the Mount. That wasn't the only time Jesus' disciples had to make an effort to experience Him more deeply:

> [1] After six days Jesus took Peter, James, and his brother John and led them up on a high mountain by themselves. [2] He was transformed in front of them, and His face shone like the sun. Even His clothes became as white as the light.
> MATTHEW 17:1-2

Once again, the disciples put real effort into following Jesus. They sacrificed their time and energy in order to be in the right place to learn from Him—and the reward was incredible.

Read the entire experience in Matthew 17:1-13. What did the disciples learn from Jesus in these verses?

When have you experienced Jesus as your Teacher?

It's not easy to follow Jesus. You'll sometimes need to scale a mountain just to hear from Him. But the effort will be more than worth it.

Unfortunately, some disciples remain at base camp at the bottom of that mountain and find great comfort in never exercising their faith, never growing, and never hearing from God. Others begin the ascent, but the demands of life (or their own bad habits) drag them down well before the summit. But the ones who complete the journey up the mountain will hear from God. And His voice will give them peace, comfort, and joy.

How will you remind yourself to make daily (or hourly) decisions to actively trust Jesus and listen for His voice?

DISCIPLES OBEY WHAT THEY LEARN

There are many scary verses in the Bible. But this verse near the end of Jesus' Sermon on the Mount may be one of the scariest:

> Not everyone who says to Me, "Lord, Lord!" will enter the kingdom of heaven, but only the one who does the will of My Father in heaven.
> MATTHEW 7:21

Maybe you're wondering, *what did Jesus mean when He said to do "the will of My Father in heaven"?* The answer is that obeying God goes beyond doing the right things. In fact, God has always been unimpressed with people who do the right things for the wrong reasons:

> 11 "What are all your sacrifices to Me?"
> asks the Lord.
> "I have had enough of burnt offerings and rams
> and the fat of well-fed cattle;
> I have no desire for the blood of bulls,
> lambs, or male goats. ...
>
> 15 When you lift up your hands in prayer,
> I will refuse to look at you;
> even if you offer countless prayers,
> I will not listen.
> Your hands are covered with blood.
> ISAIAH 1:11,15

What emotions do you experience when you read these verses from Matthew 7 and Isaiah 1? Why?

Rewrite Isaiah 1:11 based on your own experiences with church today.

During the Sermon on the Mount, Jesus proclaimed that our fruit is what separates true disciples from those who are simply going through the motions. Interestingly, Jesus wasn't teaching something entirely new. He was expanding on a similar idea from Isaiah 1.

Read Isaiah 1:16-20. What kinds of "fruit" from following God are mentioned in these verses?

Jesus' disciples also emphasized the theme of spiritual fruit when they wrote later portions of the New Testament. The most famous example came from the apostle Paul:

> [22] The fruit of the Spirit is love, joy, peace, patience, kindness, goodness, faith, [23] gentleness, self-control. Against such things there is no law.
> **GALATIANS 5:22-23**

Remember that obeying God involves more than snap decisions or brief spurts of righteousness. We don't produce fruit simply by saying, "I'm going to be kind or peaceful for a few minutes so that I can prove I love God." Instead, the fruit of the Spirit will be naturally and automatically cultivated in our lives when we genuinely follow Jesus, submit to His teaching, and grow to be more and more like Him.

In other words, we don't follow Jesus by trying to do more good things. Rather, the fruit of the Spirit provides evidence that God is working to transform our hearts.

Which elements of the fruit of the Spirit are most evident in your life?

Which elements of the fruit of the Spirit are least evident in your life?

JESUS EQUIPS HIS DISCIPLES

Jesus gives us what we need to engage
in His mission for the world.

REFLECT

We previously saw that disciples of Jesus need to intentionally adopt a posture in which they can learn from Him. In addition, we saw that the process of learning is only complete—and only results in true transformation—when it's connected to obedience in our actions. The more we learn from Jesus and obey His teaching, the more fruit we'll produce for His kingdom.

As you prepare to explore how Jesus equips His disciples, take a moment to reflect on your experiences in recent days.

Which of the assignments did you explore this week? How did it go?

What did you learn or experience while reading the Bible?

What questions would you like to ask before we move forward?

PRAY

Begin this session by connecting with God through prayer. Use the following guidelines as you speak with Him together:

- Thank God for what you've learned and experienced in recent weeks.

- Express your desire to be equipped as a participant in Jesus' mission for the world. Be honest about what you'd like to gain and where you'd like to grow in order to participate more fully.

- Ask for courage to not only understand what you encounter in God's Word this session, but also to obey what you learn.

INTRODUCTION

Do you DIY?

DIY is an acronym that stands for "Do it yourself." It refers to the phenomenon of people tackling home-improvement projects themselves whenever possible, rather than calling plumbers, carpenters, and other professionals. DIY people take pride in successfully completing a project and saving money at the same time.

Of course, there are probably millions of people who attempt to tackle home-improvement projects every week. But just attempting a project doesn't make you DIY. In fact, there's really one main difference between DIY people and non-DIY people: tools.

You can usually tell if a person is really into the DIY experience by the tools he or she uses. DIY people have learned from experience that the right tool is often the difference between a job well done and an expensive mess. For that reason, DIY people equip themselves with the tools they need to accomplish their goals.

When have you recently felt equipped to accomplish an important task, such as painting your own room, repairing a bike or a skateboard, or changing the oil in your car?

Here's a question you should consider honestly: Would Jesus give you a job to do without also equipping you to be successful? Thankfully, the answer is no.

In this session, we'll see how Jesus equipped His disciples even as He sent them out to fulfill a specific mission. This was an important moment for the early disciples, and it carries a lot of implications for us as we seek to participate in Jesus' mission for the world.

In what ways would you like to feel more equipped as you participate in Jesus' mission for the world?

KNOW THE STORY

Matthew 10 marks a turning point in the lives of Jesus' earliest disciples. Until that moment, the disciples had spent most of their time with Jesus. They traveled with Him, served with Him, ate with Him, and even celebrated with Him. In Matthew 10, however, Jesus sent them out in pairs to minister away from Him.

¹ Summoning His 12 disciples, He gave them authority over unclean spirits, to drive them out and to heal every disease and sickness. …

⁵ Jesus sent out these 12 after giving them instructions: "Don't take the road leading to other nations, and don't enter any Samaritan town. ⁶ Instead, go to the lost sheep of the house of Israel. ⁷ As you go, announce this: 'The kingdom of heaven has come near.' ⁸ Heal the sick, raise the dead, cleanse those with skin diseases, drive out demons. You have received free of charge; give free of charge. ⁹ Don't take along gold, silver, or copper for your money-belts. ¹⁰ Don't take a traveling bag for the road, or an extra shirt, sandals, or a walking stick, for the worker is worthy of his food.

¹¹ "When you enter any town or village, find out who is worthy, and stay there until you leave. ¹² Greet a household when you enter it, ¹³ and if the household is worthy, let your peace be on it. But if it is unworthy, let your peace return to you. ¹⁴ If anyone will not welcome you or listen to your words, shake the dust off your feet when you leave that house or town. ¹⁵ I assure you: It will be more tolerable on the day of judgment for the land of Sodom and Gomorrah than for that town."
MATTHEW 10:1,5-15

What emotions would you have experienced if you received these instructions from Jesus?

Which part of these instructions seems most difficult? Why?

UNPACK THE STORY
JESUS PROVIDES WHAT WE NEED

In our efforts to live as His disciples, Jesus equips us with a number of important resources. We have the Bible, for example, which serves as our foundation for understanding God, the world, and history. We also have access to the church—a community of brothers and sisters working together in service to God. And we have our own unique mix of talents and abilities.

How have your talents and abilities empowered you to participate in Jesus' mission for the world?

Still, how would you like to receive the following instructions from Jesus?

Heal the sick, raise the dead, cleanse those with skin diseases, drive out demons. You have received free of charge; give free of charge.
MATTHEW 10:8

If you don't think you could handle these commands—you're absolutely right. People don't possess such supernatural abilities on their own. The only way Jesus' disciples were able to perform these miraculous feats was because Jesus Himself had granted them His power and authority: "Summoning His 12 disciples, He gave them authority over unclean spirits, to drive them out and to heal every disease and sickness" (Matt. 10:1).

Disciples today are also called to achieve an incredible goal—the advancement of God's kingdom throughout the world. For that reason, we must never lose sight of the crucial truth that our most important resource in following Jesus is our access to Jesus Himself.

When have you felt empowered to take action or make the right choice because of your relationship with Jesus?

Jesus equipped the disciples with His power and presence in order for them to obey His commands. The great news is that He does the same for us.

JESUS CLARIFIES WHAT WE DON'T NEED

Not only did Jesus equip the disciples with His power and presence, He also made sure they understood what they *did not* need in order to carry out His mission:

> [9] Don't take along gold, silver, or copper for your money-belts. [10] Don't take a traveling bag for the road, or an extra shirt, sandals, or a walking stick, for the worker is worthy of his food.
> MATTHEW 10:9-10

Does that mean you should get rid of your suitcase the next time you go on a mission trip? Not exactly.

Jesus was calling the disciples to let go of what made them feel safe and comfortable before they went on mission. Why? Because He wanted them to rely completely on His power and presence. He wanted them to set aside their own resources so they would be free to demonstrate faith in His provision.

When was the last time you took a leap of faith? What happened next?

As modern Christians, we need to understand that what Jesus is calling us to do is far beyond our own abilities and resources. To be honest, if your concept of following Jesus fits neatly into the American dream or our culture's conception of a "normal" life, you need to stretch your understanding of what it means to be a disciple of Christ.

Following Jesus should force us to rely completely on Him.

What are your current goals as a disciple of Jesus?

In what ways have you been dependent on Jesus in order to achieve those goals?

ENGAGE

Setting goals is a good practice for most areas of life. If you want to make the team or be first chair in the band, it makes sense to start practicing ahead of time. It's also beneficial to set goals concerning your walk and growth as a disciple of Jesus. But your goals for following Christ should be vastly different than your goals for your sport or for your success in the band. Why? Because your goals as a Christian should be big, bold, and audacious. In fact, the goals you set as a follower of Jesus should be impossible to achieve without the intervention and support of Jesus.

That being the case, take a few moments to practice setting goals as a Christian. Work with your group to create short-term and long-term dreams that will connect with your passions and will force you to rely on Christ.

How would you like to grow as a follower of Christ?

Short-term goals	Long-term goals

What would you like to achieve as a follower of Christ?

Short-term goals	Long-term goals

PRAYER REQUESTS:

....

....

....

....

In addition to studying God's Word, work with your group leader to create a plan for personal study, worship, and application between now and the next session. Select from the following optional activities to match your personal preferences and available time.

⬆ Worship

☑ Read your Bible. Complete the reading plan on page 58.

☐ Connect with God each day through prayer. As you make a conscious effort to rely on God throughout the day, it's important that you stay connected with Him through regular times of prayer.

☐ Spend time with God by reading the devotion and answering the questions on page 59.

➡⬅ Personal Study

☐ Read and interact with "Jesus Provides What We Need" on page 60.

☐ Read and interact with "Jesus Clarifies What We Don't Need" on page 62.

⬅➡ Application

☐ Take a prayer walk through your neighborhood or school. As you walk in a specific area, share with God your hopes and dreams for ministering in that area.

☐ Work with your family to evaluate whether anything is holding you back from fully relying on Jesus as you follow Him. Be open to difficult decisions.

☐ Memorize Matthew 10:27-28: "What I tell you in the dark, speak in the light. What you hear in a whisper, proclaim on the housetops. Don't fear those who kill the body but are not able to kill the soul; rather, fear Him who is able to destroy both soul and body in hell."

☐ Start a prayer journal by writing down your prayer requests each day (or each week) and then recording the answer to those requests each time God responds. This is a great way to see clearly how well God provides for you.

☐ Other:

WORSHIP

READING PLAN

Read through the following passages this week. Use the space provided to record your thoughts and responses.

Day 1
Genesis 22:1-18

Day 2
Genesis 50:1-21

Day 3
Exodus 6:28–7:13

Day 4
Joshua 2:1-24

Day 5
1 Samuel 17:1-37

Day 6
John 4:1-26

Day 7
Philippians 2:1-18

MORE THAN YOU NEED

In your attempts to live as a follower of Jesus, you may have felt inadequate or unprepared in certain situations. You may even have felt ineffective or unworthy as a disciple. Perhaps you feel that way now.

Whether or not you struggle with those emotions, the truth is that you are indeed inadequate to follow Jesus in your own strength. You are unprepared based on your own knowledge. Similarly, you will be ineffective when you attempt to take matters into your own hands. And you are certainly unworthy to live as a disciple of Christ, who is your Master as well as the all-knowing, ever-present, all-powerful God.

It's not just you, though. All Christians are unable to follow Jesus in and of themselves. That's the bad news.

The good news is that Jesus has called you to follow Him in spite of your limitations. And because of His presence in your life, you are neither inadequate nor unprepared. Because He is the source of your strength, you are neither ineffective nor unworthy. You can live successfully and powerfully as a disciple of Jesus because you are connected to Him.

He's all you need!

In what ways do you feel weak or inadequate as a follower of Jesus?

In what situations, settings, or circumstances do you often struggle to live boldly and confidently as a disciple of Christ?

How will you spend time in Jesus' presence this week in order to draw strength and confidence from Him?

JESUS PROVIDES WHAT WE NEED

When we allow Jesus to be the primary source and supply for fulfilling our mission, He equips us in a number of important ways. For example, Paul wrote the following description of "the armor of God," which we receive as we are "strengthened by the Lord":

> ¹⁰ Finally, be strengthened by the Lord and by His vast strength. ¹¹ Put on the full armor of God so that you can stand against the tactics of the Devil. ¹² For our battle is not against flesh and blood, but against the rulers, against the authorities, against the world powers of this darkness, against the spiritual forces of evil in the heavens. ¹³ This is why you must take up the full armor of God, so that you may be able to resist in the evil day, and having prepared everything, to take your stand.
>
> ¹⁴ Stand, therefore, with truth like a belt around your waist, righteousness like armor on your chest, ¹⁵ and your feet sandaled with readiness for the gospel of peace. ¹⁶ In every situation take the shield of faith, and with it you will be able to extinguish all the flaming arrows of the evil one. ¹⁷ Take the helmet of salvation, and the sword of the Spirit, which is God's word.
> **EPHESIANS 6:10-17**

What do you think Paul meant by "our battle" in verse 12?

How have you benefited from the armor described in verses 14-17?

With which pieces of armor would you like to be equipped in a more powerful way?

Remember that Jesus equips us with His armor through "His vast strength." You can't will yourself into having more faith or more righteousness. Rather, just like the fruit of the Spirit, you'll be equipped with the armor of God as you intentionally connect with other Christians, study God's Word, pray, and obey Him.

We saw in Matthew 10 how Jesus sent the disciples out in pairs to minister in their communities. After the disciples returned, Jesus sought to equip them further by deepening their relationship with Him:

> 30 The apostles gathered around Jesus and reported to Him all that they had done and taught. 31 He said to them, "Come away by yourselves to a remote place and rest for a while." For many people were coming and going, and they did not even have time to eat.
> MARK 6:30-31

Don't miss this important truth: Jesus equips us with everything we need to participate in His mission for the world, but this equipping happens primarily as we spend time in His presence. That was true of Jesus' earliest disciples, and it's true of His disciples today.

How have you recently made time to connect with Jesus in a deep and personal way?

When will you make time this week to connect with Jesus?

Remember that we don't have to engage God's mission on our own. In fact, *we can't* engage God's mission on our own. We don't have the ability or the authority. But the great news is that Jesus gives us everything we need in order to participate in His mission (Matt. 10:1). We're weak, but He's strong. We're fragile, but He's powerful. We fumble over our words, but He speaks for us (Matt. 10:20). We have weak arguments, but He changes hard hearts (Ezek. 36:26).

Your mission is not your own, and your authority is not your own. All you're called to do is humbly obey.

How is God calling you to obey Him right now? (Consider spending time in prayer as you contemplate this question.)

JESUS CLARIFIES WHAT WE DON'T NEED

One of the challenges that has hindered followers of Jesus throughout history is that it's so often easier to question God's commands than to obey them. It's easier to complain than to be generous. It's easier to judge than to talk of grace or offer hope.

In other words, our hearts are great at finding excuses for why we can't participate in Jesus' mission:

- I don't know enough Scripture.

- I don't have the right gifts.

- I don't have time.

- I don't have friends who will join me.

What excuses do you use when you don't want to obey what God is asking of you?

Jesus' original disciples looked for the same excuses we do. That's why Jesus told them not to take anything extra as they set out to make an impact in their communities. (See Matthew 10:9-10.) No money to spend. No staff for protection from enemies. No extra clothes to stay comfortable if something wore out. Instead of relying on their "extras" to carry them through their journeys, Jesus commanded the disciples to rely on Him.

Which "extras" eat up a large percentage of your time and attention throughout the week?

What do you typically rely on—money, connections, family, and so on— to carry you through difficult situations?

Two stories from the Gospel of Luke highlight some additional baggage we don't need to carry when we follow Jesus. First, we don't need to retain our sense of self-importance:

> [46] Then an argument started among them about who would be the greatest of them. [47] But Jesus, knowing the thoughts of their hearts, took a little child and had him stand next to Him. [48] He told them, "Whoever welcomes this little child in My name welcomes Me. And whoever welcomes Me welcomes Him who sent Me. For whoever is least among you—this one is great."
> LUKE 9:46-48

As a follower of Jesus, you will be tempted to compare yourself to other disciples. Such comparisons are rarely helpful, and they often cause great damage.

How often do you compare yourself to other Christians?

1	2	3	4	5	6	7	8	9	10

Rarely   **Often**

The second type of baggage we don't need to carry as followers of Jesus is our self-righteous behavior and tendency to judge those with whom we disagree:

> [49] John responded, "Master, we saw someone driving out demons in Your name, and we tried to stop him because he does not follow us." [50] "Don't stop him," Jesus told him, "because whoever is not against you is for you."
> LUKE 9:49-50

How often do you stand in judgment over the way others follow Christ?

1	2	3	4	5	6	7	8	9	10

Rarely   **Often**

It's easy to fall into the trap of believing that our community is the only community that follows Jesus correctly—that we're the only ones who worship right, behave properly, believe the right doctrines, and witness the best way. The truth is, those who truly follow Christ are all servants in submission to Him as our Master and Lord.

JESUS SENDS HIS DISCIPLES

Christ calls us to take the gospel to the world.

REFLECT

So far in this study, we've learned that a disciple is a follower of Jesus Christ (Session 1), that Jesus calls His disciples to Himself (Session 2), that He teaches His disciples what it means to follow Him (Session 3), and that He equips His disciples to join Him in His work (Session 4).

As you prepare to dive deeper into the ways Jesus actively sends us into the world, take a moment to reflect on your experiences in recent days.

Which of the assignments did you explore this week? How did it go?

What did you learn or experience while reading the Bible?

What questions would you like to ask before we move forward?

PRAY

Begin this session by connecting with God through prayer. Use the following guidelines as you speak with Him together:

- Thank God for what He has taught you during this study and for the ways He has helped you grow in your knowledge of Him.

- Pray that God would bless you with the courage necessary to act on what you've learned in recent sessions, and especially on what you will learn in this final session.

- Commit now to making the most of your time as you conclude this study on what it means to live and grow as a disciple of Christ.

INTRODUCTION

As a stunt man for Universal Studios, Michael Brady specialized in skydiving. During a filming session in Benson, Arizona, Michael was preparing to parachute onto the top of a moving train when he slipped and fell from a high elevation. He struck his head on landing and died instantly.

That wasn't the end of his story, however. Michael's body was taken to the University Medical Center in Tucson, where his heart was removed and transplanted into the body of another man, Bill Wohl, who had suffered heart failure more than five months before.

Six months and one day after receiving his new heart, Bill Wohl opened a letter from Michael Brady's family, which included a picture of Michael and some background information. Bill was shocked to learn he'd been given the heart of a 36-year-old Hollywood stuntman. "I looked at this picture," Bill said, "at this incredibly good-looking, super-fit, super-athletic guy. And I thought: *Are you kidding me? That's whose heart I've got?*"

Before his heart transplant, Bill Wohl had been a Type A, overweight, money-obsessed businessman pursuing a jet-setter lifestyle. Today he works part time, spending most of his new-found energy winning speed and performance medals in swimming, cycling, and track.

When interviewed by a reporter in his Scottsdale condo, Bill Wohl spoke passionately about the blessing he'd received: "Every day, all day, I thank God for Michael Brady." Glancing at his many medals won through athletic competitions, Wohl added, "When I ride, when I work out—the biggest thing is to honor him."

In other words, Bill Wohl was dramatically changed by a new heart.

What are the biggest changes you've experienced in your time as a follower of Jesus?

Like Bill Wohl, you have received a new heart as a disciple of Jesus. You are in the process of being transformed from the inside out. When Christ's heart beats in your chest, you will live to honor Him each day and you will share His passion to take the gospel to the world.

KNOW THE STORY

Jesus' earliest disciples experienced a roller-coaster ride during the final weeks of His public ministry. First, Jesus' death on the cross sent them into confusion and deep despair. Second, His resurrection lifted them back into the clouds of joy. Finally, His ascension ushered in the sobering reality that the disciples would continue carrying out Jesus' mission without His physical presence and leadership.

Before Jesus returned to heaven, however, He gathered His remaining followers in order to summarize the mission for His disciples and deliver final instructions. Today we refer to Jesus' final words as the Great Commission.

> [16] The 11 disciples traveled to Galilee, to the mountain where Jesus had directed them. [17] When they saw Him, they worshiped, but some doubted.
>
> [18] Then Jesus came near and said to them, "All authority has been given to Me in heaven and on earth. [19] Go, therefore, and make disciples of all nations, baptizing them in the name of the Father and of the Son and of the Holy Spirit, [20] teaching them to observe everything I have commanded you. And remember, I am with you always, to the end of the age."
> MATTHEW 28:16-20

What are your first reactions to these verses? Why?

In what ways has this commission been carried out in the centuries since Jesus sent His earliest disciples?

In what ways is Jesus' commission still incomplete?

The Great Commission summarized Jesus' mission not only for His earliest disciples, but also for all of the disciples who have joined the ranks of His followers throughout history—including you. We'll conclude this study by taking a close look at Jesus' commission and command for those who choose to follow Him.

UNPACK THE STORY
JESUS TELLS US WHERE TO GO

The first thing to highlight about Jesus' statements in these verses is His claim to authority. Why is it important that "all authority in heaven and earth has been given" to Jesus? Because His Great Commission is a series of commands. He is ordering us to obey Him. Therefore, He first wanted to state clearly that He carries the authority to do so.

What does it mean to recognize Jesus' authority in our lives?

Next, the Great Commission has a geographical connection. Jesus commanded us to "Go, therefore, and make disciples of all nations." First, notice that Jesus' command is active rather than passive. He didn't command His disciples to think about the world. He didn't ask His followers to say nice things about different people groups. Jesus commanded His disciples to "Go."

This doesn't mean all Christians should serve as international missionaries. However, it does mean all Christians should take an active role in spreading the gospel throughout the world—and it certainly means we should be open to the possibility of physically traveling to other places to spread the gospel.

Have you been involved in missions through your church? If so, how?

Second, notice that Jesus' command involves "all nations." Jesus died for the sins of all people, which means the gospel has power for every tribe and nationality across the world. We cannot forget that Jesus has commanded us, His disciples, to proclaim the gospel message to all who need to hear it.

To ignore the spiritual needs of people outside our own country is to disobey the Great Commission and ignore what Christ has commanded.

What are different ways we can obey Jesus and contribute to spreading the gospel across "all nations"?

JESUS TELLS US WHAT TO DO

Not only did Jesus tell us where to participate in His mission, but He also gave us a clear process through which we can carry out that mission:

> [19] Go, therefore, and make disciples of all nations, baptizing them in the name of the Father and of the Son and of the Holy Spirit, [20] teaching them to observe everything I have commanded you.
> **MATTHEW 28:19-20**

This process is key to understanding our mission as followers of Jesus. We are called to make disciples, and we start by proclaiming the gospel wherever we can. When our efforts produce fruit—when someone makes a decision to follow Jesus—baptism is the next step. To be baptized is to publicly announce yourself as a follower of Christ.

If you've accepted Christ as your Savior, have you been baptized? If so, what was that experience like for you?

Unfortunately, many Christians believe this to be the end of the process—that once a person "gets saved" and is baptized, there's nothing left to do. Jesus told us differently in His Great Commission. When we proclaim the gospel and begin the process of making disciples, we are responsible for "teaching them to observe everything" He has commanded us.

Certainly this kind of "teaching" involves helping people learn information about God and His Word—but it also goes way beyond information. When we teach people to "observe" what Jesus commanded, we teach them to obey. And the only real way to teach obedience is to model what needs to be obeyed. In other words, one of our main goals in living out the Great Commission is to connect with new disciples in such a way that we provide an example of how to follow Christ.

Who has been an example of Christlikeness for you?

How confident do you feel in your ability to make disciples and serve as an example for others to follow?

ENGAGE

When Christians think about Jesus' command to "make disciples of all nations," we often get stuck on the idea of physically traveling to foreign lands. That is certainly part of what Jesus meant, and it is important for us to keep an open mind about full-time and part-time missions work. However, there are many other ways to engage the mission of making disciples throughout the world.

For example, prayer is one of the best tools available for joining Jesus in His mission for the nations. Prayer is both easily accessible and powerfully effective. It can't be stopped by restricted borders or corrupt governments. And prayer works in our lives, as well, to keep us connected with God.

Take a minute to practice praying for the nations as a group. To get started, look on the tag of your shirt—or your shoes, if that's easier—to see in which country it was manufactured. Use the following guidelines to pray for God's kingdom to move forward in that country.

Pray for the churches and Christians currently living in your selected country. Pray for their safety and their ability to share the gospel.

Pray against any corruption or religious persecution that threatens your fellow disciples.

Pray for new opportunities to share the gospel in your country and to meet the needs of those who live there.

PRAYER REQUESTS:

....

....

....

....

....

....

....

....

In addition to studying God's Word, work with your group leader to create a plan for personal study, worship, and application between now and the next session. Select from the following optional activities to match your personal preferences and available time.

↑ Worship

☑ Read your Bible. Complete the reading plan on page 72.

☐ Spend time with God by reading the devotion and answering the questions on page 73.

☐ Connect with God each day through prayer. Ask Him to provide opportunities for you to participate in His mission of making disciples.

➡ ⬅ Personal Study

☐ Read and interact with "Jesus Tells Us Where to Go" on page 74.

☐ Read and interact with "Jesus Tells Us What to Do" on page 76.

⬅ ➡ Application

☐ Make an effort this week to connect with people who have not experienced salvation through Jesus Christ. Break your normal routine and make an effort to talk with them about Jesus.

☐ Make a list of people in your life whom Jesus may be leading you to disciple. Pray through that list each day.

☐ Make a list of people who would be good candidates to disciple you (or to serve as a mentor). Pray through that list each day.

☐ Memorize Acts 1:8: "You will receive power when the Holy Spirit has come on you, and you will be My witnesses in Jerusalem, in all Judea and Samaria, and to the ends of the earth."

☐ Other:

↑ WORSHIP

READING PLAN

Read through the following passages this week. Use the space provided to record your thoughts and responses.

Day 1
Mark 16:1-20

Day 2
Luke 10:1-16

Day 3
Luke 24:36-53

Day 4
John 20:1-31

Day 5
Romans 10:1-21

Day 6
Romans 16:1-27

Day 7
2 Corinthians 10:1-18

THE FEAR OF FAILING

Our fears often hold us back from obeying Jesus and fulfilling His Great Commission. We can become fearful of many things, such as:

- Looking foolish

- Not knowing the answers to questions

- Being rejected

- Being called out for our own sin, and much more

Basically, we're afraid of failing. And these fears aren't irrational. In fact, these and other fears will come true time and time again if we commit to making disciples. We will be rejected. We may look foolish even to ourselves. We'll trip and fall over the truth. But remember this truth: We never fail when we choose to obey God. This is true even when we don't have all of the "right" answers—even when we're rejected, scorned, neglected, and despised.

In fact, when we're rejected and despised, we're a lot like Jesus.

On the other hand, never forget that to abandon our commission—to refuse to go, share, give, and speak—is to have already failed. We don't have to be the ones who control the outcome and change people's hearts. All we have to do is obediently go as our Savior sends us out. The choice is ours.

What makes you feel afraid at the thought of sharing the gospel with the people in your life?

When has fear prevented you from fulfilling Jesus' commission?

What specific steps will you take to own your fears and overcome them?

JESUS TELLS US WHERE TO GO

We know that Jesus has called us to join Him in a crucial mission: the redemption of the world. We also know He has the authority to call us into action:

> Then Jesus came near and said to them, "All authority has been given to Me in heaven and on earth."
> **MATTHEW 28:18**

To have authority means having the power to give orders to others—and having the ability to see those orders carried out to completion. In other words, someone with authority can both enact and enforce a rule. Therefore, Jesus' claim to authority means He can send us out into the world.

But here's the great news: Jesus' authority also means we carry His power and credentials when we go out into the world to do His work. In other words, we aren't proclaiming the gospel and making disciples based on our own names or our own abilities. Instead, we've been sent by the One who holds the keys to both heaven and earth.

This takes the pressure off of us because Jesus is the One who makes things happen. Jesus is the One who changes hearts, minds, and habits. Jesus is the One who convicts people of their sin. Jesus is the One who redeems the world. All we need to do is be faithful to obey His command: "Go."

Have you been relying on Jesus' authority or on your own abilities during your efforts to make disciples?

1	2	3	4	5	6	7	8	9	10

My own abilities   **Jesus' authority**

What steps can you take to lean more heavily on Jesus' authority?

Now that we understand the basic question of authority behind Jesus' command to "Go," we must still obey Jesus' commission. In Matthew 28, He called the disciples to "make disciples of all nations." Immediately before His ascension, Jesus clarified the different places we should go in our efforts to make disciples.

[7] He said to them, "It is not for you to know times or periods that the Father has set by His own authority. [8] But you will receive power when the Holy Spirit has come on you, and you will be My witnesses in Jerusalem, in all Judea and Samaria, and to the ends of the earth."
ACTS 1:7-8

In what ways do you need the Holy Spirit to help you be Jesus' witness both at home and "to the ends of the earth"?

The places Jesus referenced move outward geographically. They start in close proximity and move further away. Jerusalem was the place closest to where Jesus spoke these words; it was the central city for both the Jews and the earliest Christians. Judea was the name of the region that included cities like Jerusalem, Bethlehem, and Joppa. It was a broader area. Samaria was the region to the north, and it was noteworthy because the Samaritan people and the Jews were enemies—they were different in terms of race and religion.

You probably don't live in any of those places, but Jesus' call still applies to you. How? Your "Jerusalem" includes the people closest to you; it's your family, friends, neighbors, and coworkers. Your "Judea" is your larger community, including the people in your county, state, and country. Your "Samaria" is the people who are around you but not like you—those who are different from you.

Finally, don't ignore Jesus' command to be witnesses "to the ends of the earth." All disciples of Christ have a responsibility to think internationally as we follow Him and make disciples.

Who are some people you can serve from the following groups?

Your "Jerusalem":

Your "Judea":

Your "Samaria":

"The ends of the earth":

JESUS TELLS US WHAT TO DO

We've seen that Jesus gave us the process through which we can participate in His mission for the world by making disciples of all nations:

> [19] Go, therefore, and make disciples of all nations, baptizing them in the name of the Father and of the Son and of the Holy Spirit, [20] teaching them to observe everything I have commanded you. And remember, I am with you always, to the end of the age.
> MATTHEW 28:19-20

The process involves four steps:

Go. We go into the world to sew the seeds of the gospel through our words and deeds.

Make disciples. When the Holy Spirit causes those seeds to grow in the lives of those we know, we help them respond to God through recognizing their sin and turning from it.

Baptize them. We help new disciples connect with the body of Christ through the public declaration of their faith.

Teach them to observe Jesus' commands. We walk in partnership with new disciples to help them learn the truths of God's Word, apply those truths, and begin making disciples themselves.

Which of these steps do you find most difficult or intimidating? Why?

As members of the church, we often feel as if our "job" is done when a person reaches step 3 and makes a public declaration of faith in Jesus. It's not.

To be sure, what we refer to as "salvation" or "justification" is an incredible moment in the life of a disciple—it's the moment during which a person moves from death into life. Likewise, baptism is a wonderful event that should be celebrated by all members of the church.

However, there is much more work to be done. Our commission from Jesus involves continually teaching new and established disciples what it means to follow Him. We are commanded to participate in the sanctification of others even as we experience sanctification ourselves.

Use the questions below to help think about your own journey through the process of discipleship. Also work to identify the ways you're investing in this process today in the lives of others.

How have you benefited from other followers of Jesus during each of these four steps?
Go:

Make disciples:

Baptize them:

Teach them:

How are you currently helping others follow Jesus through each of these four steps?
Go:

Make disciples:

Baptize them:

Teach them:

DISCIPLESPATH

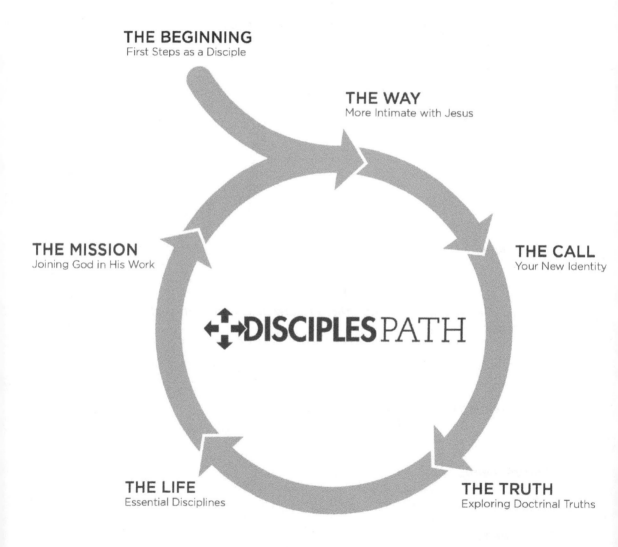

THE BEGINNING
First Steps as a Disciple

THE WAY
More Intimate with Jesus

THE MISSION
Joining God in His Work

THE CALL
Your New Identity

DISCIPLESPATH

THE LIFE
Essential Disciplines

THE TRUTH
Exploring Doctrinal Truths

TAKE THE NEXT STEP.

Disciples Path is a series of resources founded on Jesus' model of discipleship. Created by experienced disciple makers across the nation, it is an intentional path of transformational discipleship. While most small-group studies facilitate transformation through relationship and information, these disciple-making resources do it through the principles of modeling, practicing, and multiplying.

- Leaders model a biblical life
- Disciples follow and practice from the leader
- Disciples become disciple makers and multiply through *Disciples Path*

Each of the six studies in the *Disciples Path* series has been written and approved by disciple makers for one-on-one settings as well as small groups. The series includes:

1. THE BEGINNING
Take the first step for a new believer and new disciple, exploring the foundations of following Jesus and discovering the answers to questions that all disciples ask.

2. THE WAY
Walk through the Gospels and follow the journey of Jesus and the first disciples.

3. THE CALL
Gain a deeper understanding of what it means to follow Christ in everyday life.

4. THE TRUTH
Dive into the doctrinal truths of biblical discipleship.

5. THE LIFE
Take a deeper look at the essential disciplines and practices of following Christ.

6. THE MISSION
Get equipped for God's mission and discover your role in joining Him in the world.

To learn more or take the next step, visit lifeway.com/disciplespath.

LEADER INSTRUCTIONS

As a group leader or mentor, you have a vital role in the process of discipleship—one that involves both blessing and responsibility. Keep in mind the following guidelines as you faithfully obey the Great Commission.

YOUR GOAL

Remember that your ultimate goal in the discipleship process is spiritual transformation. The best fruit for your efforts as a leader is spiritual growth that results in transformed hearts—both for you and for the disciples under your care.

Remember also that spiritual transformation is most likely to occur when a godly leader applies truth to the heart of a person while that person is in a teachable posture. As the leader, you have direct control over the first two of those conditions; you can also encourage and support disciples as they seek a teachable posture. Take advantage of those opportunities.

YOUR METHODS

Use the following suggestions as you work toward the goal of spiritual transformation.

- **Pray daily.** Studies have shown that leaders who pray every day for the disciples under their care see the most spiritual fruit during the discipleship process. Your ultimate goal is spiritual transformation; therefore, seek the Holy Spirit.

- **Teach information.** This resource contains helpful information on the basic elements of the Christian faith. During group discussions, you'll want to be familiar enough with the content to avoid reading each page verbatim. Highlighting key words or even creating your own bullet points will help you facilitate the time most effectively. Prepare in advance.

- **Seek conversation.** As you lead disciples through the material, seek to engage them in meaningful conversation. To help you, discussion questions have been provided throughout the group portion of each session. These questions provide an opportunity to pause and allow each disciple to react to the teaching. They also allow you as the disciple-maker an opportunity to gauge how each person is progressing along the path of discipleship.

- **Model practices.** Many disciples learn best by observing others. Therefore, each session of this resource includes opportunities for you to model the attributes, disciplines, and practices of a growing disciple of Jesus. Take advantage of these opportunities by intentionally showing disciples how to pray, interact with God's Word, worship God, and so on—and by inviting feedback and questions.

May God bless your efforts to guide others toward the blessing of new life through Christ and continued transformation through His Spirit.